AMERICAN NATURE GUIDES
BIRDS OF PREY

AMERICAN NATURE GUIDES
BIRDS OF PREY

PHILIP BURTON
TREVOR BOYER
Malcolm Ellis
David Thelwell

GALLERY BOOKS
An Imprint of W. H. Smith Publishers Inc.
112 Madison Avenue
New York City 10016

This edition first published in 1991 by Gallery Books,
an imprint of W. H. Smith Publishers, Inc.,
112 Madison Avenue, New York, New York 10016

Published in England by Dragon's World Ltd, Limpsfield and London

Editor: Martyn Bramwell
Designer: Tom Deas
Series Design: David Allen
Editorial Director: Pippa Rubinstein

Gallery Books are available for bulk purchase for sales promotions and
premium use. For details write or telephone the Manager of Special Sales,
W. H. Smith Publishers, Inc., 112 Madison Avenue, New York,
New York 10016.
(212) 532 6600

ISBN 0 8317 6950 5

Typeset Apple Macintosh by Flairplan Limited

Printed in Singapore

Contents

CARACARAS AND FALCONS 113

INDEX 142

Introduction

From the earliest times, birds of prey have occupied a special place in man's feelings toward the natural world. At times his attitudes have appeared favorable, and the aerial hunters have been seen as symbolizing freedom, power, and nobility. Conversely, birds of prey have equally often been perceived as a threat, and have been persecuted mercilessly as a result. Neither attitude really does the birds justice, however, and only now are they coming to be valued for their own sake, as superbly adapted living creatures, often endowed with great beauty, and with fascinating ways of life. If this book helps to foster a true appreciation of them, coupled with a concern for their future, then it will have achieved its object.

CLASSIFYING THE BIRDS OF PREY

Hopefully it should be possible to open this book anywhere and find interesting reading coupled with fine illustrations, but in order to understand the birds of prey more fully it is helpful to have a working knowledge of how birds and other living things are classified and named. First of all, terms such as "birds of prey" and "raptor" need to be explained. In the broadest sense, any bird that takes animal food, be it the tiniest insect, could be described as a bird of prey, but in practice the term is usually reserved for those that capture prey that is large in proportion to their own size. Usually this will be vertebrate prey – chiefly reptiles, mammals, and other birds, but sometimes also fish and amphibians. Even here a difficulty arises because some other groups of birds, such as herons, gulls and crows, take similar animals. All these, however, capture and kill their prey with the bill. True birds of prey have the feet and claws developed into formidable talons to perform these tasks; in most species the intimidating hooked bill is for tearing up food rather than for killing it in the first place.

Following these criteria then, the term "birds of prey" is normally understood to include the hawks, eagles, vultures, falcons and allies, and the owls. The first set are grouped together in a single Order called the Falconiformes; these are the day-active birds of prey, also called "raptors", with which this book is concerned. The owls, the nocturnal birds of prey, are classified in a separate Order, Strigiformes. This implies that the two are not considered to be closely related, and that their similar features have evolved independently. Such judgments about relationships are based on very detailed studies of anatomy, behavior, and biochemistry which try to chart the course taken by evolution. The various levels of grouping therefore aim to reflect ancestry rather than merely overall similarity of features.

Below the level of Order, the next main unit of classification is the Family. Within the Order Falconiformes, five families are recognized – the Cathartidae, Pandionidae, Accipitridae, Sagittariidae and Falconidae. Two of these – the Pandionidae and Sagittariidae – contain just one species each. Surprising as this might seem at first, it is necessary in order to recognize the many unique and fundamental features which set them apart from the larger families.

Continuing down the scale of classification, the next main level of grouping is the Genus, and this leads us into a consideration of nomenclature, as the name of the genus is also the first part of the scientific name of each species. A genus may include only one species if it has no close relatives, or it may include a large number of species. The largest raptor genus, for example, is *Accipiter*, which contains 47 species, all sharing a very similar body plan and way of life. Each species is given a scientific name consisting of the genus name first, followed by the species name; the whole usually being printed in italics. Thus, the Sharp-shinned Hawk bears the name *Accipiter striatus*, while a similar species in Eurasia, the Sparrowhawk, is called *Accipiter nisus*.

THE SPECIES ACCOUNTS
In this pocket guide, a standard approach has been taken to the individual species entries. For each species the male bird is illustrated in color, in full breeding plumage and in a pose characteristic of the bird. On the species distribution maps, tint areas show the year-round range of resident birds and the breeding range of migrants, with solid lines of color indicating the limits of distribution of migrant birds outside the breeding season.

    The concise summary text is presented under a series of headings covering identification features, habitat preferences, nesting habits, food preferences, range, and any known seasonal movements. At the top of each entry there is a data panel giving the bird's

The American Kestrel (*Falco sparverius*) is the only New World kestrel. It is found from Canada south to Tierra del Fuego.

average dimensions and weight, and details of the clutch size, eggs, and incubation and fledging periods. Size information is not complete for all species, but in accordance with current widespread practice two dimensions are given wherever possible. Length is that of the bird on its back, from bill tip to tail tip, a condition normally only attainable with a dead specimen. As it is prone to subjective error in measuring it is not available for all species, but it does give some indication of general size. The other measure, wing length, is widely used in ornithology due to its greater precision. It refers to the distance from the wrist joint of the wing to the tip of the longest flight feather. Wing length should not be confused with wing-span, which is the distance between the two wing tips when the wings are fully stretched out. This is the measurement most people are interested in, but unfortunately it is even more prone to error than body length, and is consequently available only for a small proportion of species. Accordingly it has been omitted here, but as a rough guide, the span of many large soaring birds of prey is about three times the wing length.

Individuals vary in size in all species, but where this variation is not large, a single median value is given. For many species, however, it is necessary to give a size range. This may be due to geographical variation, but more usually it is due to size difference between the sexes. Interestingly, in most birds of prey it is the female that is the larger, and the difference is most marked in many bird-eating species. It is least marked in scavenging species, and in some vultures particularly, the males are somewhat larger, as in the majority of birds. It has been suggested that the usual greater size of females is necessary to enable them to establish the dominance that causes the males to bring food throughout incubation and much of the fledging period. The size difference may also have some safety value during courtship, so strong are the aggressive urges of the male.

THE FLIGHT CHARACTERISTICS OF RAPTORS
Much interest is shown in the powers of flight displayed by birds of prey, although there is often some misunderstanding on this topic. High speed, as demonstrated by falcons such as the Peregrine, for example, is not by any means a universal characteristic of raptors; indeed some are actually specialized for flying extremely slowly. Taking the group as a whole, the range of wing shape and mode of flight is very wide indeed. In comparing them, key factors to be considered are wing loading, aspect ratio, and the shape of the primaries or main flight feathers.

Wing loading is a simple enough concept; it is simply the relationship between body weight and wing area. Birds that have a large wing area relative to their weight are said to have low wing loading, and vice versa. Among birds of prey, harriers have the lowest wing loading at some 0.41 to 0.61 pounds per square foot. Unspecialized birds of prey such as buzzards stand at around 0.82 to 0.90 pounds per square foot; sparrowhawks and goshawks at about 1.1 pounds per square foot, and large falcons at about 1.43 pounds per square foot. In general, higher wing loadings are associated with more rapid flight, and this is especially true for birds such as falcons, which attain maximum speed in a dive. Highest loadings of all, however, are found in large eagles and vultures. Although their huge wings have a very large area, their bodies are proportionately heavier still, and wing loading can be as high as 2.46 pounds per square foot. The very low wing loading of harriers is related to their method of hunting, which involves quartering a stretch of ground very slowly and systematically. As they do this they are not only looking for prey but also listening for it, as hearing is especially highly developed in this group.

Aspect ratio is the ratio of wing length to wing breadth. Short, broad wings have low aspect ratios; long narrow ones have high aspect ratios. High aspect ratios are most suited to soaring and gliding, but in their most extreme form, as in albatrosses, they make take-off slow and difficult and cause proportionately more turbulence, so that a high air-speed is required. Soaring raptors such as vultures and some eagles have wings a good deal broader than this to permit slower flight with greater maneuverability. Very low aspect ratios are typical of forest species, which may have to weave in and out of trees at high speed as they pursue their prey.

The shape and relative length of the primary flight feathers affects the whole appearance and functioning of the wing tip. Swift species such as the falcons have pointed wing tips, but in many species the shape is

Swainson's Hawk (*Buteo swainsoni*) breeds on the Great Plains and winters on the Argentine pampas.

more rounded, and the feathers themselves may have a "cut-away" outline so that their tips appear widely separated, like splayed fingers. Particularly strongly marked in large soaring species, this feature helps smooth the air flow over the wing, a vital factor when air-speed is slow. The "alula", a bunch of feathers attached to the vestigial thumb of the wing skeleton, has a similar effect, and functions rather like the flaps that are deployed as an aircraft comes in to land.

Soaring species, when not migrating, are generally using their high vantage-point to look for ground-living prey or carrion. The same is generally true for those species that "still hunt", that is, watch for prey from a perch. Raptors that take their prey in flight have attracted particular interest, however, and careful studies of falconers' birds using high-speed cinematography have clarified the technique they employ. It is the large falcons and the accipiters (sparrowhawks and goshawks) that specialize most in this type of hunting, falcons typically attacking in a dive or "stoop", while accipiters generally attack in level flight. Both, especially the falcons, are traveling very fast when they overtake their prey, but this speed is primarily concerned with bringing them into a killing position. What then happens is that the pelvis and legs are swung at the prey, adding greatly to the force of the blow. Peregrines in fact level out and slow down somewhat as they strike, and in any case deliver only a glancing blow with the open feet. This is still enough to cause instant death in most cases: were the strike any harder, the falcon would endanger its own limbs, to no good purpose. I have so far avoided being struck by a raptor, but have twice been the target for a Tawny Owl, which uses a similar technique. Such a blow feels like a direct hit from a brick, and one is astonished that it can have come from a bird weighing little more than a pound.

THREATS TO THE BIRDS OF PREY

Concern over environmental issues is now a prominent feature of current affairs, and birds of prey illustrate very clearly some of the key problems in conservation. The relationship between the numbers of prey and the number of predators is one of the most crucial of these. One of the chief reasons why birds of prey have so often been persecuted is their supposed depletion of stocks of game. This ignores the fact that under natural conditions it is the numbers of prey that control the numbers of predators, and not the other way about. Thus, if two grouse moors of equal size are hunted respectively by one pair of eagles and by two pairs, it can be confidently predicted that the moor with the extra eagles has substantially *more* grouse on it, not less. The only exceptions to this occur when numbers of predators are maintained at an artificially high level by some human activity such as the disposal of offal or garbage, which provides a large supplementary food source. This type of problem occurs more commonly with such predators as gulls than with raptors.

Birds of prey are, indeed, much less numerous than most of the smaller species they feed on, but because they are relatively large and conspicuous this fact is often overlooked. It does, however, make them much more vulnerable to persecution or environmental hazards. Where pollutants are concerned, an additional problem is that although the chemicals are initially widely dispersed, they accumulate in ever greater concentrations as they move upward through a food pyramid, and birds of prey which generally stand at the top of such pyramids may receive them in dangerous concentrations. For this reason, birds of prey can serve as valuable indicators of the health of our environment, and studies of their breeding success and ecology play a prominent role in monitoring the impact of modern technology on the world we live in.

New World Vultures

Family CATHARTIDAE

Turkey Vulture

Cathartes aura

Length:	25in	**Eggs:**	2; white or cream, heavily	
Wing:	21in		mottled reddish-brown	
Weight:	1lb 15oz –	**Incubation:**	38 – 41 days	
	4lb 6oz	**Fledging:**	75 – 80+ days	

Identification: The all-black plumage, with some blue, green, and purple iridescence, and the rather small, unfeathered red head, with white bill, make this species easy to identify. However, it is most often seen on the wing, and when viewed from below, the silvery-gray primaries, contrasting with the generally dark appearance, and the long tail, extending beyond the pale fleshy-white legs and feet, make it unmistakable. The bird has a characteristic flight-profile, the wings being held in a shallow "V", with virtually no flapping, while progress is usually effected by buoyant side-slippings.

Habitat: The Turkey Vulture is the most widespread species of its family, and occurs in a variety of habitats, including desert, open plains and plateaux, forests, and jungle.

Nest: No real nest is built: the birds lay their eggs in caves

(preferably with two entrances), hollow logs or tree-stumps, a suitable depression in a swamp, or hidden in a dense thicket. What, if any, nest-material exists is gathered from the immediate surroundings, and may consist of rotten wood from inside a tree-hole, dead leaves on the ground, or even hay or straw on the rare occasions when the birds choose to nest in an old shed. Such material appears simply to form a cushion for the eggs.

Food: The Turkey Vulture has the most highly developed sense of smell of any member of its family, which means it is always first to arrive at a potential food-source. Carrion of all sorts, from fresh to putrid, is taken with equal relish. The bird seems to prefer small animals, but nothing remotely edible is refused. It will also eat rotting fruit and vegetables and, very occasionally, the nestlings and eggs of other birds. Claims that it takes livestock are virtually groundless.

Range: The Turkey Vulture is found throughout North America as far north as southern Canada.

Movements: Southerly fall migrations of Turkey Vultures are mostly from the arid western parts of the range and the higher altitudes of northern Mexico, and cover vast distances down into South America. Nevertheless, even though they may reach speeds of up to 40 mph, the birds seem to expend little energy on such journeys due to their ability to cover considerable distances on motionless wings. The birds return in early spring, and both overland journeys are often made in company with huge numbers of Swainson's and Broad-winged hawks.

Yellow-headed Vulture
Cathartes burrovianus

Length: 30in

Wing: 19in

Weight: 2lb 12oz

Eggs: ? 2; whitish, blotched red-brown and pale gray

Incubation: ? 40 days

Fledging: ? 80+ days

Identification: The generally green-glossed black plumage of the Yellow-headed Vulture is set off by the brightly-colored head and neck, which are usually some shade of yellow or

orange, often mixed with red, and by a bluish tinge on the crown. Further contrast is provided by the off-white legs, feet, and outer primary quills.

Habitat: The species shows a definite liking for damp situations, including grasslands, marshes, savannas, and even broken woodland in the vicinity of water.

Nest: This species' nesting habits are presumed to be similar to those of the Turkey Vulture, but little evidence exists at present. A pair is said to have nested in a hollow trunk, at about 12 feet above ground level.

Food: Fish figures strongly in the Yellow-headed Vulture's diet, and probably includes some live individuals taken when stranded in shallow water. In common with other vultures, it will feed on virtually all types of carrion, and there is some evidence to suggest that it also takes insect larvae and other invertebrates.

Range: This species occurs locally in savanna country toward the east coast of Mexico. It also ranges southward through Panama, and has a huge South American distribution extending from the north, down across almost all of Brazil.

Movements: Although migration in this species has yet to be proved, it seems probable that many birds move south for the dry season. Certainly there is an increase in numbers at that time of year in, for example, Venezuela, and if there is an influx of birds, they are more likely to have come from the north than from the south.

Black Vulture
Coragyps atratus

Length:	22in	**Eggs:**	2; pale gray-green, sparsely
Wing:	17in		blotched brown
Weight:	2lb 9oz -	**Incubation:**	32 - 39 days
	4lb 4oz	**Fledging:**	70+ days

Identification: As its name implies, this vulture is entirely matt black, including the bare skin on the head and neck, although some individuals may have a purplish sheen to the head, wings, and tail, while the pale-tipped bill, eyes, and feet are all dark brown. The undersides of the primaries are white, and form a distinctive underwing patch when the bird is observed in flight.

Habitat: The Black Vulture is a bird of semi-open and wooded country, with a strong attraction to any human habitation where easy pickings of refuse and offal are to be had. This is particularly so in South America, where the species occurs in huge numbers around shanty towns, slaughterhouses, and fishing harbors.

Nest: No nest is built. The birds select a cave; a low hollow tree or stump, rarely more than 15 feet above ground; a hollow beneath rocks or thorny scrub; or occasionally a cavity on a large building, in which to lay their two eggs. Occasionally the

species nests socially, but this seems to be a result of nest-site scarcity rather than true colonial nesting. Young Black Vultures in the nest defend themselves by bill-snapping and uttering hoarse cries and hisses. Older young also disgorge their stomach contents when disturbed.

Food: The species' main diet is carrion, offal, and excrement of all types, together with eggs and overripe or rotten fruit and vegetables, but occasionally it will also kill young or helpless animals, including domestic stock. For this reason, and the fear that it is a transmitter of disease, it has been trapped and slaughtered in thousands, notably in Texas. Black Vultures do not find food by smell like Turkey Vultures, but are attracted to food sources discovered by the latter. The Black dominates the Turkey at a carcass, but is itself dominated by the considerably larger King Vulture. Some vegetable matter is also consumed, and the species is also attracted to offshore islands with seabird colonies or turtle breeding beaches, both a source of helpless young prey.

Range: The Black Vulture is probably the most numerous of any Western Hemisphere vulture. It ranges south from Washington State, across the southern part of Ohio to southern Arizona, and as far as Mexico. It also extends through Central America as far as central Patagonia.

Movements: Although considered sedentary, flocks of this species have been seen moving south through Panama during November, which is considerably later than the migration of the Turkey Vulture.

King Vulture

Sarcorhamphus papa

Length:	30in	**Eggs:**	1; unmarked white
Wing:	19.5in	**Incubation:**	56 - 58 days
Weight:	7lb 12oz	**Fledging:**	? 90+ days

Identification: The head of the King Vulture, with its wattle, extraordinary wrinkled facial skin, and intricate color-pattern of yellow, orange, purple, and blue, combine with the white eye to make it totally unmistakable. The back plumage is vinaceous-buff with a gray neck-ruff, the wings and tail are black, and the underparts white.

Habitat: Most commonly the species is found in extensive lowland rainforest, although it is sometimes to be found in savanna grasslands, and also in cattle-grazing country.

Nest: Virtually nothing is known of the King Vulture's nesting habits although it is reputed to lay its single egg in a hollow trunk or rock-crevice, more or less at ground level.

Food: Carrion of all types forms the bird's diet. Being the largest and often most numerous species at any corpse, other vultures always yield to it, even when the King arrives late. Claims that it kills both wild and domesticated animals need verification.

Range: In Mexico, the species is found from the Isthmus of Tehuantepec, eastward across to the lower part of the Yucatan Peninsula. It is also occasionally seen as far north as Veracruz. In South America it ranges as far south as northern Argentina.

Movements: There is no evidence that the species undertakes any migratory movements.

California Condor

Gymnogyps californianus

Length:	49in	**Eggs:**	1; greenish- or bluish-white, unmarked	
Wing:	34in	**Incubation:**	42 - 52 days	
Weight:	18 - 31lb	**Fledging:**	200+ days	

Identification: Due to its immense size the California Condor is unmistakable. Except for a few scattered black, bristly feathers, the head and neck are bare; the head-skin is usually some shade of orange, merging into pale gray on the neck, but these tints may vary, possibly in response to the bird's mood. The general plumage is blackish, with an untidy neck-ruff of long, pointed feathers; the back feathers are edged with brown, and the primaries with gray. In flight, the underside shows a white wing-bar, formed by the white underwing coverts, and white-edged secondaries. Adults have pinkish legs, a whitish bill, and a red eye. It is highly improbable that any observer

will now see this virtually extinct species anywhere in the wild. All known individuals are now in "protective custody" in California zoos.

Habitat: The dry west-coastal areas of California, up to about 8,000 feet, and their associated open plains, are now the only habitat likely to still hold wild individuals of this almost extinct bird.

Nest: No nest is built: the single egg is laid in the sand or other accumulated material on the floor of any cave large enough to accommodate the birds. A narrow part is always selected, which, in a large cave, may be as much as 30 feet from the entrance. Exceptionally, a cavity high up in a giant sequoia may be used. The birds have a number of alternative sites, which are used in a somewhat haphazard sequence.

Food: The California Condor is essentially a scavenger, feeding on carrion of all types but preferring larger carcasses such as deer, cattle, and horses. The species has never been known to kill living animals.

Range: Although formerly occurring over a much wider area, unwarranted persecution and reduced food availability have now restricted the species' range to central and southwestern coastal areas of California, and it may well be extinct in the wild. Some 25 or so individuals are currently held in captivity, and any offspring from these birds would appear to offer the only hope for the species' survival.

Movements: The California Condor is not known to migrate. Any local movements are almost certainly in response to reduced food availability.

OSPREY

Family PANDIONIDAE

Osprey
Pandion haliaetus

Length:	22in	**Eggs:**	3 (2 - 4); white, marked with	
Wing:	19in		brown and gray	
Weight:	2lb 11oz -	**Incubation:**	32 - 33 days	
	4lb 3oz	**Fledging:**	50 - 60 days	

Identification: The male Osprey has a white head, with a dark brown crown and a broad, blackish eye-stripe; the remainder of the plumage is deep brown above, white below. The eye is pale

yellow, and the legs and feet greenish-white. The female is similar, but has an upper-breast band of brown streaks.

Habitat: The most usual place to find Ospreys is near reasonable-sized lakes and rivers, or the sea. The presence of large trees, or rocky outcrops, on which the birds can perch between hunting forays, seems to be an added requirement.

Nest: The nest is a large, rather untidy, grass-lined structure made of sticks, which the birds snap off trees by grasping them with the feet as they fly past. It is usually sited on top of a tree or crag, and sometimes even on a telegraph pole. Increasingly, the birds are building on pole-mounted platforms erected specially for them. The nest is used, and added to, for many years, and may become as much as five feet in diameter, and almost as high.

Food: Although items such as crustaceans and birds occasionally figure in the Osprey's diet, its food consists almost entirely of fish, up to four pounds in weight, which are captured in spectacular fashion. The bird hovers, up to 100 feet above the water, then plunge-dives, feet first, onto its prey, often becoming almost totally submerged. The fish is then carried off, held head-forward in the feet, which are positioned one behind the other.

Range: In North America the Osprey ranges from Alaska down to California, across the continent to the east coast, and north to Newfoundland.

Movements: The species migrates south, to winter in Mexico, the West Indies, and parts of South America.

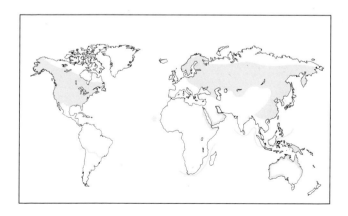

KITES, VULTURES EAGLES AND HAWKS

Family ACCIPITRIDAE

Cayenne Kite
Leptodon cayanensis

Length: 19.5in

Wing: 12.5in
Weight: 17 - 21oz

Eggs: 2 (3); grayish-white, speckled reddish-brown

Incubation: not recorded
Fledging: not recorded

Identification: The gray head, blackish upperparts contrasting with white underparts, and long, white-barred tail should easily identify this species.

Habitat: The Cayenne Kite is usually found in humid lowland or subtropical forests, often in the vicinity of water, but the bird is sometimes seen along marsh edges, and in drier savannas.

Nest: Unfortunately, the nest has never been positively identified; however, a nest thought to belong to this species was found high in a tree, and was constructed with small twigs.

Food: The Cayenne Kite takes a wide variety of food, including insects of many orders, mollusks, birds' eggs (which it swallows whole), and amphibians. One individual was observed pecking pieces from a still-wriggling snake, indicating that it may occasionally capture larger prey. Its fondness for wasp larvae, which are often consumed in large numbers (along with wax and bits of comb), indicates its affinities with the Honey-Buzzards *(Pernis)*.

Range: The bird is distributed southward from east-central Mexico into eastern Bolivia, northern Argentina, Paraguay, and southern Brazil. It is also found on Trinidad.

Movements: The bird is apparently nonmigratory: certainly no long-distance movements have been recorded.

Hook-billed Kite
Chondrohierax uncinatus

Length:	16in	**Eggs:**	2; white, with chocolate-brown blotches
Wing:	11in	**Incubation:**	not recorded
Weight:	8.8 - 10.5oz	**Fledging:**	not recorded

Identification: The sexually dimorphic Hook-billed Kite has a number of color phases, individual and age variants, and variations in bill dimensions. The most usual form of the male is slaty-gray above, with a white tip to the tail, and with the underparts barred gray and white. The female pattern is similar, but rufous-brown rather than gray, and with a rufous collar. In both sexes the bill is heavy, with a pronounced hook to the upper mandible.

Habitat: Usually found in tropical and subtropical zones up to around 6,000 feet above sea level, the Hook-billed Kite tends to be somewhat unobtrusive, often secreting itself in the lower forest canopy or in dense undergrowth. It is sometimes found in small groups of two or three.

Nest: The twig-lined nest of sticks, broken off with the bill, is sited in a tree, about 30 feet above the ground, and is built by both sexes.

Food: Snails of many species are the bird's preferred diet, the hooked bill enabling the fleshy parts to be extracted efficiently and cleanly. Other recorded prey-items include frogs, salamanders, and insects.

Range: The species occurs in tropical parts of Texas and Mexico, but is nowhere very common.

Movements: The Hook-billed Kite is not known to migrate, but occasionally ventures out into open areas, including swamps and marshes.

Swallow-tailed Kite

Elanoides forficatus

Length:	24in	**Eggs:**	2 (4); off-white, boldly blotched dark brown
Wing:	16.5in	**Incubation:**	28 days
Weight:	13.7 - 15.8oz	**Fledging:**	36 - 42 days

Identification: The long, deeply forked tail and graceful flight easily identify this beautiful species. The back, wings, and tail are deep bluish-black, contrasting strongly with the pure-white head and underparts. The bill is black, the eye brown to reddish, and the legs and feet pale bluish-gray.

Habitat: Although most commonly found in cypress swamps, the Swallow-tailed Kite is also known to frequent areas of pines.

Nest: The well-constructed nest is always sited at the top of a tall, slender tree, and is made of twigs broken off in flight and then transferred to the bill for building. The nest measures up to 20 inches across, and has a lining of Spanish moss.

Food: The Swallow-tailed Kite is an aerial feeder par excellence, catching flying insects with one foot and then transferring them to the bill. Other prey-items, such as lizards, snakes, or pieces of wasp's nest, are similarly taken in flight. This bird has even been known to snatch a whole nest, and devour the nestlings in it, one by one, without ever alighting. Drinking is also performed on the wing, water being scooped up swallow-fashion.

Range: Formerly found as far north as Minnesota, the species is now mainly restricted to Florida, with a few breeding pairs scattered along the Atlantic coast as far as South Carolina. However, it is nowhere common.

Movements: Among the earliest of migrants in both spring and fall, most Swallow-tailed Kites overwinter in South America, with some occasionally passing the winter in Florida.

White-tailed Kite
Elanus leucurus

Length:	15in	**Eggs:**	4 - 5; white, richly blotched brown	
Wing:	12in	**Incubation:**	28 days	
Weight:	10oz	**Fledging:**	35 - 40 days	

Identification: With the exception of the white forehead, the entire upperparts are pearly-gray, with jet-black shoulder patches. The underparts are pure white. The white tail, from which the species derives its name, is noticeable only when in flight, for only the outer feathers are white, and these are hidden by the gray central feathers when the bird is at rest. The bill is black, the eye reddish-orange, and the legs yellowish-buff. This is the only North American kite that hovers when hunting.

Habitat: The bird is found in most kinds of open countryside, including semi-arid areas.

Nest: The flimsy-looking but nevertheless well-built nest is made of dry twigs, broken off with the bill, often after a considerable tussle. It is lined with dry grass and straw. The nest is placed near the top of a tree, site selection and most of the construction being the duty of the female.

Food: Mice and other small mammals form the bulk of the species' diet but this is supplemented with small birds, amphibians and lizards, as well as with large insects which, apparently, are always taken on the ground.

Range: The White-tailed Kite is locally distributed from South Carolina to California, where it is most numerous. The population seems to be on the increase, and the range expanding.

Movements: Although some South American populations are migratory, North American birds move only locally, in response to fluctuating rodent numbers.

Snail Kite
Rostrhamus sociabilis

Length:	18in	**Eggs:**	3 - 4; heavily blotched with brown
Wing:	14in	**Incubation:**	26 - 28 days
Weight:	10.5 - 14oz	**Fledging:**	23 - 28 days

T. BOY

Identification: The adult male Snail Kite is entirely slaty-black, except for the white tail coverts, and a white tail with a broad dark band and paler tip. The eyes, facial skin, legs, and feet are orange-red. The female is similar, but dark brown rather than black, and is grayish-white on the forehead and throat. The bill, with its long, fine hook, is distinctive in both sexes.

Habitat: Watercourses and freshwater marshes of southern Florida are the restricted habitat of this species in North America.

Nest: The Snail Kite's nest, sited anywhere between 3 and 16 feet above water, in bushes or marsh grasses, is a relatively small and untidy collection of twigs and sticks. Nests are often close together, forming small colonies.

Food: The bird's diet consists exclusively of apple snails *(Pomacea)*, which are plucked from the water with one foot, carried to a favored feeding-post, and then efficiently dealt with using the highly specialized bill.

Range: Although very common and widespread in many parts of South America, the Snail Kite is sparsely distributed and not at all common in its restricted southern Florida haunts.

Movements: The Snail Kite is resident in Florida throughout the year, its specialized diet precluding any long-distance movements.

Mississippi Kite
Ictinia misisippiensis

Length:	14in	**Eggs:**	2 (1 - 3); unmarked, bluish-white
Wing:	12in		
Weight ♂: 8.6oz		**Incubation:** 31 - 32 days	
Weight ♀: 11oz		**Fledging:** 34 - 35 days	

Identification: The male Mississippi Kite has the head, back, and underparts pearly-gray, with the mantle and wings slaty-gray, merging into blackish. The tips of the secondaries are white, forming an indistinct wing-bar, and the inner primaries are often partially rufous. The tail is also blackish, and unmarked. The eye and the legs are orange-red. The female is similar, but somewhat darker.

Habitat: The Mississippi Kite's choice of habitat is extremely varied, ranging from continuous forest through to open prairie, and even virtually barren landscapes. At least some trees within reasonable distance seem to be necessary in order for the bird to breed.

Nest: The nest, sited in a tree-fork at any height between 10 and 75 feet above ground, may be a disused crow's nest, the birds' own nest from a previous season, or the pair may opt to construct an entirely new one. The often flimsy structure is built of twigs, broken off with the bill while perched, or with the feet, following a dive. It is often rather oval in shape, usually built by the female (with material gathered by her mate) and has a shallow lining of green leaves. Nests are sometimes so numerous as to form a loose colony.

Food: The species feeds on all types of flying insect, which it captures in the feet with almost nonchalant ease while on the wing. Such prey is often eaten in flight, the wings being discarded at the time of eating while the chitinous parts are cast up later, as pellets. There is some evidence that the Mississippi Kite also snatches small lizards and frogs from treetops, as well as taking bats in flight.

Range: Now found locally from Kansas and Iowa across to South Carolina and down to northwestern Florida. The species formerly bred as far north as southern Illinois and Indiana.

Movements: The Mississippi Kite is highly migratory, being recorded, outside the breeding season, as far south as Paraguay and even northern Argentina. The few individuals previously thought to be breeding in Mexico and Central America are now generally considered to have been on passage. It seems that the birds select their mates during the return flight, for they are always paired up on arrival at their breeding sites.

Bald Eagle
Haliaeetus leucocephalus

Length:	33 - 43in	**Eggs:**	2 (1 - 3); unmarked,
Wing:	20 - 27in		dull white
Weight ♂:	9lb 11oz	**Incubation:**	30 - 46 days
Weight ♀:	13lb 13oz	**Fledging:**	70 - 80 days

Identification: With its massive yellow bill and pure-white head and tail, contrasting with the otherwise black-brown plumage, the Bald Eagle cannot be confused with any other species.

Habitat: Although most often seen in watery locations, such as sea-coasts or in the vicinity of rivers or lakes, the species is occasionally seen along mountain ridges, particularly when on migration.

Nest: The enormous nest, which is added to annually over many years, is always sited in a commanding position, either in a tree or on a rock outcrop. It is constructed of deadwood, either collected from the ground or snapped off trees in flight, with a lining of some softer material, pine needles often being selected. Green sprays are added to the nest throughout the breeding cycle.

Food: The bird eats a variety of fish, birds, and mammals, and although it hunts and catches much live prey, which it certainly seems to prefer, it appears forced, at times, to resort to carrion. Claims that it causes reductions in domestic lamb and salmon stocks are greatly exaggerated: the birds almost invariably take only sick, dying, or even dead, animals.

Range: The Bald Eagle is distributed over continental North America, as far south as southern Florida and the coast of Baja California, Mexico. Unfortunately, as a result of persecution, pollution, and human disturbance, the species is now really common only in Alaska, the more southerly populations having been severely depleted.

Movements: The Bald Eagle has a somewhat erratic migration pattern. Most, but not all, northern birds move south once the expanses of water begin freezing over. Curiously, however, many Florida-based birds move north for the summer, traveling as far north as the northeastern United States and southern Canada. This may be because reduced food supplies during the hottest months are insufficient to support the whole population.

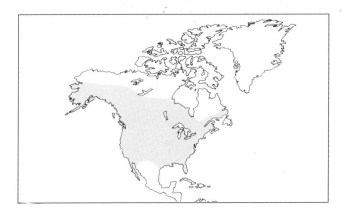

White-tailed Sea Eagle
Haliaeetus albicilla

Length: 27 - 36in
Wing: 22 - 28in
Weight ♂: 8lb 14oz
Weight ♀: 11lb 5oz

Eggs: 2 (1 - 3); dull white, sometimes stained yellow
Incubation: 35 - 45 days
Fledging: 70 days

BOYER

Identification: The most obvious feature, from which the bird derives its name, is the pure-white, unmarked tail. The rest of the plumage is yellow-brown above and below, becoming darker toward the tail, and with the primaries grayish. The heavy bill, eyes, and legs are yellow.

Habitat: Remote sea-cliffs, deep, inhospitable river valleys, and sometimes large, isolated inland lakes are the haunts of the White-tailed Sea Eagle.

Nest: The birds prefer to build their huge nest in a large tree, usually more than 60 feet above the ground, but where no trees are available they will select a rocky crag, or even a low hummock. The birds have several alternative nests, which may be added to at any time, and which, after several years, can become huge structures of branches and twigs measuring six feet across by ten feet deep. The deep central cup is lined with greenery, and sometimes wool.

Food: Fish, either picked up dead or plucked live from the water surface, form the bulk of the species' diet. It will also take waterbirds, up to the size of a swan, and even mammals, from rat-size up to Roe Deer fawns. It is not averse to feeding on carrion, although this is never offered to the young.

Range: This basically Eurasian species is a rare visitor to the Outer Aleutians, where it has been known to nest.

Movements: The species is a partial migrant, some pairs remaining on station all year round while others move south at the onset of cold weather to winter in India and the Chinese region. Exceptionally, Eurasian birds will travel as far as Africa.

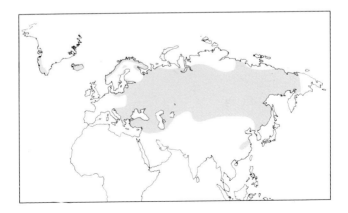

Steller's Sea Eagle
Haliaeetus pelagicus

Length:	42 - 44.8in	**Eggs:**	2 (1 - 3); white, with slight greenish tinge
Wing:	22 - 27in		
Weight ♂:	12lb 2oz	**Incubation:**	38 - 45 days
Weight ♀:	18lb 8oz	**Fledging:**	70 days

Identification: The massive orange-yellow bill, and pure-white shoulders, thighs, and tail, contrasting with the otherwise black-brown plumage, easily identify this huge eagle. The eye, cere, and legs are all yellow. Immatures lack the white shoulder patches, and have a dark band across the tail.

Habitat: Rocky sea-coasts, and tree-lined rivers with extensive flood plains within easy reach of the sea.

Nest: The enormous nest, constructed of branches and sticks, may be as much as 8 feet across and 12 feet deep. It is sited in or on top of a tree, up to 100 feet above the ground. Usually only one young is reared, but up to three have been recorded.

Food: A wide variety of prey is taken by Steller's Sea Eagle, including large fish, birds up to the size of geese, mammals from leverets to seal pups, and crabs and mollusks. It is also known to take carrion, and like the Bald Eagle it is attracted to salmon rivers to feed on dead and dying spent fish. Immatures in winter sometimes scavenge for offal in the vicinity of slaughterhouses.

Range: The species is normally found along the north Pacific coast of the USSR, and in suitable areas in North Korea.

Movements: Steller's Sea Eagle migrates to northern Japan and Korea for the winter, and at this time occasionally arrives as a straggler on the Aleutian, Pribilof, and Kodiak Islands. Spectacular gatherings of this magnificent species are to be seen on ice floes off northern Japan in winter.

Crane Hawk

Geranospiza caerulescens

Length:	17 - 20.8in	**Eggs:**	? ; plain white
Wing:	11 - 13in	**Incubation:**	not recorded
Weight:	12.3oz	**Fledging:**	not recorded

Identification: The Crane Hawk is a slim, overall grayish-black hawk, with a long tail crossed by two broad white bands. At rest, the very long orange legs are noticeable, as is the red eye, while a narrow white underwing band is visible in flight.

Habitat: The species shows a distinct preference for the vicinity of water, wherever there is at least a strip of cover. It also inhabits woodland interspersed with small streams and pools, and is occasionally found in forested swamps.

Nest: The nest is usually sited in a tree, at between 30 and 55 feet above ground. It is a small, rather open cup of twigs and vine stalks, lined with grasses, fine twigs, and some green leaves.

Food: The Crane Hawk feeds on lizards, tree frogs, snakes, large insects, and birds' eggs and nestlings, all of which it captures in an almost unique way. The bird alights on a tree-trunk or limb, and spreading and flapping its wings to maintain stability it commences a methodical clambering search of every crack, fissure, and cavity. Since the bird's "knee" joint is capable of bending forward, as well as back, the Crane Hawk is able to probe right inside such hiding places, and extract any suitable prey. It has even been known to insert its head into a cavity, and extract prey using its bill.

Range: The Crane Hawk is found in tropical lowlands of Mexico, but has an extensive South American range throughout which it exhibits considerable geographical variation.

Movements: The Crane Hawk is not known to make any significant migratory movements.

Northern Harrier

Circus cyaneus

Length:	17 - 20in	**Eggs:**	5 (4 - 6); bluish-white,
Wing:	13 - 16in		sometimes brown-blotched
Weight ♂:	16.5oz	**Incubation:**	29 - 39 days
Weight ♀:	20oz	**Fledging:**	35 - 40 days

Identification: With his soft pearl-gray plumage, contrasting black primaries, and white rump and underparts, the male Northern Harrier is a stunningly beautiful bird. The female is duller, with a brown back, and similarly-colored spots and streaks on the underside, although she, too, has a white rump.

Habitat: Although found in many habitats, the Northern Harrier seems to prefer low-lying wetlands, open fields, and young conifer plantations.

Nest: The nest, usually in some hollow protected by vegetation, is made of small sticks, and various reeds and grasses. It varies in diameter from about 15 inches in dry situations to up to 3 feet, by several inches deep, in wet locations.

Food: The species preys mainly on small songbirds and their fledglings, voles, and leverets and young rabbits, but it will also take frogs, small reptiles, and some insects.

Range: The Northern Harrier is distributed across the greater part of North America down to northwestern Mexico, and it breeds throughout most of this area.

Movements: In fall, Northern Harriers migrate singly, heading south to Central America and Cuba, and occasionally to Colombia. Interestingly, males depart later than females and immature birds, but return earlier.

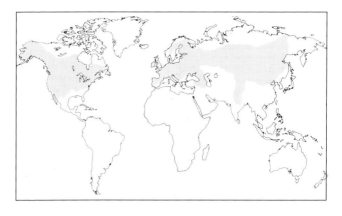

Northern Goshawk

Accipiter gentilis

Length:	18.8 - 26in	**Eggs:**	3 (1 - 5); unmarked
Wing:	12.5 - 15in		pale blue or dirty white
Weight ♂:	1lb 15oz	**Incubation:**	36 - 38 days
Weight ♀:	2lb 7oz	**Fledging:**	80 - 90 days

Identification: The adult male has the back and wings blue-gray, shading into blackish on the crown. The white underside is finely and closely barred with gray, and the white-tipped tail is crossed by a number of white-edged, broad, wavy bands. The female is similar, but brownish rather than gray.

Habitat: Generally, this is a bird of dense woodland, with a distinct preference for conifers.

Nest: The nest, which may be an old one refurbished or a new structure, is a large, untidy collection of dry sticks and twigs, either broken off by the bird's weight or bitten off with the bill. Sometimes there is a lining of green conifer sprigs and pieces of bark. The birds usually site the nest between 30 and 60 feet above ground level in a large tree.

Food: The species feeds on birds and mammals up to the size of Black Grouse (to which it is particularly partial) and young hares. Occasionally nestling songbirds are taken, the bird returning time and again until the nest is completely empty.

Range: The Northern Goshawk is rather thinly distributed across much of northern and northwestern America, and is absent from relatively treeless parts of the east and southeast.

Movements: The species is a partial migrant, with some northern areas being vacated every winter when the birds move either to the western seaboard or to the southeastern limits of the range, probably as a response to reduced food availability rather than climatic conditions.

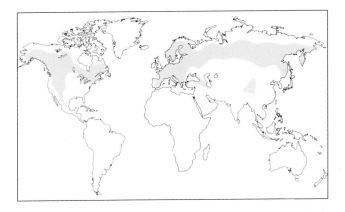

Sharp-shinned Hawk
Accipiter striatus

Length:	9.7 - 14in	**Eggs:**	4 - 5; bluish-white to white, mottled brownish
Wing ♂:	6.5 - 7in		
Wing ♀:	7.5 - 9in		
Weight ♂:	3.7oz	**Incubation:**	35 days
Weight ♀:	6.3oz	**Fledging:**	24 days

Identification: A dashing small hawk, often seen only fleetingly as it weaves swiftly between trees or bushes in pursuit of prey. The entire upperside is bluish-gray, though darker on the crown, and the white-tipped tail has three distinct gray bars. The variable underside is usually rufous or tawny, mottled and barred with white.

Habitat: The species is found in a variety of habitats, and at widely differing elevations, but it is always a bird of forested country, and shows a marked preference for conifers.

Nest: Although deciduous trees are sometimes selected, the nest is most often sited in a conifer, at the point where a number of horizontal limbs meet the trunk. It is a relatively large structure, built of twigs and lined with bark.

Food: The species' main diet consists of small birds, although it will also take small mammals, as well as lizards and insects. The female is larger and capable of dealing with rather bigger prey than her mate. It is bold and relentless in pursuit of prey, agile and maneuverable in flight, and adept at using cover to secure the advantage of surprise when attacking.

Range: From the northern tree limit of North America, down to South Carolina and Alabama.

Movements: Birds breeding in northern and central North America migrate south as far as Costa Rica. Concentrations of this species are one of the spectacular sights at Hawk Mountain, Pennsylvania, on fall migration. They pass by either flapping or sailing and soaring, sometimes indulging in aerobatics. Young birds predominate in early fall, adults later: over 1000 in a day have sometimes been counted.

Cooper's Hawk
Accipiter cooperii

Length:	14 - 20in	**Eggs:**	4 - 5; pale sky blue,
Wing ♂:	8.5 - 9.3in		rarely lightly spotted
Wing ♀:	9.7 - 11in		
Weight ♂:	13oz	**Incubation:**	36 days
Weight ♀:	20oz	**Fledging:**	30 - 34 days

T.BOYER

Identification: In the male, the crown is black, with the nape feathers showing white bases; the rest of the upperparts are leaden gray, with the tail showing three black bands and a white tip. The white underside is heavily and irregularly marked with brownish-rufous. The female is similarly marked but is browner.

Habitat: The bird is always closely associated with woodland, and usually breaks cover only when hunting.

Nest: Sited at least 30 feet up in a tree, most commonly a conifer, the nest is built almost exclusively by the male. It is constructed of twigs, which are grasped by the feet while in flight, and are broken off by the bird's weight and momentum. Before and during incubation the cup is lined with bark.

Food: Cooper's Hawk takes a variety of prey including lizards, amphibians, and large insects, but its main diet consists of birds such as flickers, meadowlarks, thrushes, and starlings. Mammals as large as squirrels and chipmunks are also taken, and since she is considerably larger than the male, the female is able to deal with prey up to the size of Ruffed Grouse.

Range: The species' range extends from southern Canada down throughout the entire United States as far south as Florida and Texas.

Movements: Cooper's Hawk is a partial migrant, with some individuals moving as far south as Costa Rica. There is even a record from Colombia of a bird banded in Manitoba.

White Hawk
Leucopternis albicollis

Length:	19 - 22in	**Eggs:**	1 - 2; white, sometimes
Wing ♂:	13 - 14.3in		with brown marks
Wing ♀:	14 - 15.5in	**Incubation:**	not recorded
Weight:	23oz	**Fledging:**	not recorded

Identification: The White Hawk is a large, strikingly white buzzard-like bird, with some black barring on the outer primaries, and a black subterminal tail-band. The eyes, legs, and feet are yellow. The race found from Mexico to Nicaragua is the whitest form and has yellow eyes, but three others are known from other parts of the New World tropics which are dark eyed and have more extensive black bars and marks on the upperparts. The only other bird conceivably likely to be confused with it (and only at long range) is the King Vulture, but in addition to its much greater size, this species has considerably more black on the flight feathers.

Habitat: The species is a bird of mixed tropical forest, with a particular liking for well-watered or swampy areas. It is most often met with in clearings, or along forest edges, but can also be seen cruising and wheeling low over the forest canopy.

Nest: The few nests so far discovered have been sited in large trees, up to 80 feet above the ground. They are built of twigs, with a lining of both dead and green leaves.

Food: The bird seems to prefer reptiles such as snakes and lizards, although individuals have been recorded as taking small mammals (up to the size of a rat), fiddler crabs, weak or incapacitated birds, and, very occasionally, insects. The White Hawk is a sluggish bird which hunts largely by watching for reptiles from a dead tree perch, usually by a clearing or a dry stream bed, and pouncing on prey when sighted.

Range: The White Hawk is found in southern Mexico, from Oaxaca through southern Veracruz to Chiapas.

Movements: This principally South American species is not known to migrate.

Common Black Hawk

Buteogallus anthracinus

Length:	18 - 22in	**Eggs:**	1 (1 - 3); grayish-white, spotted light brown
Wing:	15.5in	**Incubation:**	not recorded
Weight:	2lb 1oz	**Fledging:**	not recorded

Identification: The Common Black Hawk is entirely sooty black, with a grayish cast; the tail shows broad central, and narrow terminal, white bars. The cere, legs, and feet are bright yellow.

Habitat: The species is found most commonly in coastal lowlands of mixed savanna with patches of water and grassland, and also along wooded rivers and streams, but seldom, if ever, in dense woodland.

Nest: Almost any large tree is selected as a site for the nest, which may be placed anywhere between 15 and 100 feet above ground. It is built with a base of stout sticks, broken off in flight, mixed with smaller sticks and other suitable material and lined with twigs and some greenery.

Food: Land and sea crabs are the bird's favorite food, but it will also take frogs, fish, reptiles, and, occasionally, large insects such as grasshoppers. Small mammals are also taken, but small birds rarely figure in the diet.

Range: The species is found from southern Utah, down through Arizona, across New Mexico into Texas, and down to Mexico. In some coastal localities it is easily the commonest hawk, while in other areas, such as southern Texas, it is extremely rare.

Movements: Northern birds migrate south outside the breeding season, temporarily increasing the size of the more southerly populations.

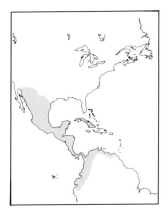

Mangrove Black Hawk

Buteogallus subtilis

Length:	not recorded	**Eggs:**	not recorded
Wing:	13in	**Incubation:**	not recorded
Weight:	not recorded	**Fledging:**	not recorded

Identification: The Mangrove Black Hawk is similar in appearance to the Common Black Hawk *(B. anthracinus)*, but is smaller, shows a much broader central tail-band, has varying amounts of rufous on the secondaries, and more extensive yellow facial skin. Individuals with bleached "washed-out" plumage are not uncommon.

Habitat: The bird is found only in mangroves, where it is said to frequent sandbars and mudflats as well as areas of denser vegetation.

Nest: The nest of this species seems never to have been recorded, but is presumed to be similar to that of the Common Black Hawk.

Food: Crabs appear to be the bird's main food, although individuals have also been observed stalking sandbars and mudflats in search of stranded or dead fish. Food is also located by perching concealed among foliage and dropping onto prey. A reported technique for dealing with crabs is to grasp the victim's legs and claws in one of the talons, and while holding it thus, to insert the hooked bill under the front of the crab's carapace and rip it off.

Range: As its name implies, the species is confined to mangrove zones, and is therefore found only along the Pacific coast of southern Mexico. It is also found in similar locations as far south as northwestern Peru.

Movements: The bird is not known to migrate, its somewhat specialized habitat precluding such an undertaking.

Great Black Hawk
Buteogallus urubitinga

Length:	20 - 24in	**Eggs:**	? 1; pale blue, heavily spotted red-brown
Wing:	15.5in	**Incubation:**	not recorded
Weight:	2lb 14oz	**Fledging:**	not recorded

Identification: This large hawk is slaty-black, with white upper tail coverts. The tail has basal, broad central, and narrow terminal white bands. There is usually some white barring on the thighs, and the legs and feet are orange-yellow.

Habitat: The bird seems to prefer moist or wet situations, and is usually found at damp forest edges, or in the vicinity of forested or wooded rivers, streams, or pools. It also occurs in mangroves and along the sea coast.

Nest: The nest is always sited in a tree, at between 25 and 40 feet, occasionally higher. It is made of sticks, with a deep cup lined with dead leaves.

Food: In common with other members of the genus, the Great Black Hawk feeds mainly on crabs. It does, however, show a liking for snakes, frogs, lizards, and small mammals, and will occasionally also take small birds and eggs, large insects, and even carrion. Relatively long legs are an aid to this species when hunting, as it drops through reeds, or snatches aquatic prey from submerged vegetation. It will seek prey in low-level flight, like a ponderous harrier, and sometimes searches for fleeing animals round the edges of grass fires.

Range: In Mexico the species occurs in all suitable habitats southward from Sonora.

Movements: As with other members of its genus, the species is nonmigratory.

Black Solitary Eagle
Harpyhaliaetus solitarius

Length:	26 - 28in	**Eggs:**	? 1; rough-textured, unmarked white
Wing:	19 - 20.5in	**Incubation:**	not recorded
Weight:	not recorded	**Fledging:**	not recorded

Identification: This large eagle is grayish to blackish, with a slight crest on the nape. The upper tail coverts are tipped with white, and the tail has prominent central, and narrow terminal, white bands. The eyes, legs, and feet are pale yellow.

Habitat: The bird is found on middle or lower mountain slopes, between 1,000 and 8,000 feet above sea level.

Nest: The bulky nest, which may measure as much as three feet in both diameter and depth, is built of stout twigs, with a lining of greenery. The few nests that have been discovered were all in Mexico, and were sited in large trees (usually conifers) at heights in excess of 250 feet. One nest was said by a local man to have been used for 45 years.

Food: Virtually nothing is known of the species' feeding habits, but a nesting pair was observed constantly carrying snakes, while many snake remains, together with those of a chachalaca *(Ortalis sp.)*, were found at another nest site. An old record refers to a pair of Black Solitary Eagles harrying fawns.

Range: The bird is very rare and sparsely distributed in Mexico from southeastern Sonora to Chiapas. As its name implies, it is almost always met with singly.

Movements: This rare and local species shows no migratory tendencies.

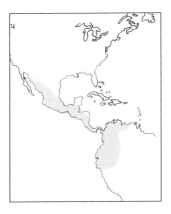

Fishing Buzzard
Busarellus nigricollis

Length:	18 - 20in	**Eggs:**	? 1; grayish-white, spotted red-brown
Wing:	14 - 16in		
Weight ♂:	16oz	**Incubation:**	not recorded
Weight ♀:	25oz	**Fledging:**	not recorded

Identification: This strikingly-plumaged species has a whitish head and a black half-collar on the upper breast. The rest of the plumage is bright chestnut, with black primaries and black tail-bars, the last one very broad. The eyes are reddish-brown, and the legs bluish-white.

Habitat: Because it is specially adapted for fishing, the Fishing Buzzard is always encountered close to water, either fresh or brackish, in open or semi-open country.

Nest: The nest is a large structure of sticks, sometimes decorated with green foliage, and is sited some 35 to 45 feet up in a mangrove or other tree, sometimes in a plantation but most often at the edge of a swamp.

Food: Prey is almost exclusively fish. The bird is also known to prey on lizards, snails and small rodents, and some aquatic insects, but all these are presumably taken only when fishing is poor.

Range: The bird's Mexican distribution extends locally down the Pacific coast lowlands from Sinaloa, and along the Gulf coast from Veracruz to Campeche. It occasionally occurs on the Yucatan Peninsula.

Movements: The Fishing Buzzard is strictly nonmigratory.

Harris's Hawk

Parabuteo unicinctus

Length:	19 - 22in	**Eggs:**	2 - 4; white, sometimes lilac- or brown-spotted
Wing:	12 - 15.5in	**Incubation:**	30 days
Weight:	not recorded	**Fledging:**	40 - 42 days

Identification: The general plumage color of this species is sooty-brown to black, with bright chestnut on shoulders and thighs, and white on the rump and tail-tip. The cere, eyelids, and legs are bright yellow.

Habitat: Semi-desert and dry sparse woodland, often in the vicinity of damp or wet areas, seem to be the species' preferred habitats.

Nest: The nest is a small, often flimsy, platform-like structure of sticks, twigs, weeds, and roots, with a lining of greenery, moss, and bark. The birds select almost any suitable tree, and usually place the nest less than 30 feet above ground level.

Food: Mammals from the size of rats up to full-grown rabbits, and medium-sized birds such as flickers, ducks, gallinules, rails, and guans, have all been recorded as prey of this species. It probably also takes lizards, but the claim that it feeds on carrion requires confirmation.

Range: The species is found, in suitable habitat, from southwestern Louisiana to Kansas, southeastern California and Texas, and down into Mexico, where it occurs in Baja California and many other areas south to Veracruz and Chiapas.

Movements: Harris's Hawk is not known to migrate.

Gray Hawk
Buteo nitidus

Length:	15 - 17in	**Eggs:**	2 (1 - 3); unmarked, white to pale bluish
Wing:	9 - 10.5in		
Weight ♂:	14oz	**Incubation:**	?26 days
Weight ♀:	22.5oz	**Fledging:**	?30 days

Identification: As its name suggests, the Gray Hawk has an overall gray appearance, but with close white barring on the underparts, and a blackish tail crossed by incomplete basal, conspicuous central, and narrow terminal white bands. The rump is also edged with a U-shaped white band. The cere and legs are yellow.

Habitat: Forest edges and lightly-wooded areas, most often in the proximity of water, are the usual haunts of the Gray Hawk.

Nest: The small, well-built nest of twigs, with a lining of green sprigs, is sited between 35 and 90 feet above the ground, almost always in a large tree. Even when the chosen tree is in the open, the nest is always well concealed in the foliage.

Food: Swifter and more agile on the wing than other members of its genus, the Gray Hawk specializes in capturing fast-moving lizards, although birds, snakes, mammals, and large insects are also taken.

Range: This tropical species is sparsely distributed in southeastern Arizona and southern New Mexico, becoming more common in the coastal lowlands of Mexico.

Movements: The Gray Hawk is not known to make any migratory movements.

Roadside Hawk

Buteo magnirostris

Length:	14 - 16in	**Eggs:**	2 (1); whitish, with rust-brown spots
Wing:	8 - 11in	**Incubation:**	not recorded
Weight:	10 - 11oz	**Fledging:**	not recorded

Identification: The upperparts are grayish brown, becoming darker on the primaries, while the tail is almost pure gray, with four black bars. The breast is grayish rufous, and the underparts are barred dusky gray and brown. The eye is yellow to orange-red, and the legs and feet are yellow.

Habitat: The Roadside Hawk is a bird of fairly open and scrubby country, found also along streams in savanna, open woodland, and forest edges. It is found at lower elevations, where it frequently lives up to its name by perching on roadside poles, posts, or wires, waiting for suitable prey.

Nest: The bulky nest of sticks, with a shallow cup lined with dry leaves, is built in a small tree, between 20 and 25 feet above ground.

Food: Although fledgling birds and small mammals are occasionally taken, the Roadside Hawk preys mainly on lizards, scorpions, insects, and spiders. It frequently attends grass fires to seek fleeing prey, and often scorches its plumage in the process.

Range: The species is found south and east from Central Mexico, extending into much of South America.

Movements: The Roadside Hawk is resident in its favorite haunts throughout the year, and is not known to make any migratory movements.

Red-shouldered Hawk
Buteo lineatus

Length:	18 - 24in	**Eggs:**	3 (4 - 5); whitish, blotched brownish
Wing:	13in		
Weight ♂:	19.5oz	**Incubation:**	28 days
Weight ♀:	25oz	**Fledging:**	35 - 40 days

Identification: The upperside is generally blackish brown, mixed with some rufous coloring which becomes more concentrated on the shoulder, where it forms a distinct patch. The wings also show narrow white barring, as does the rufous underside, while the black tail shows three white bands and a narrow white tip.

Habitat: This is a bird of wet or swampy woodland, both mixed and deciduous, as well as wooded river valleys and adjacent open country.

Nest: Although the species may sometimes use the abandoned nest of a crow or similar species, it usually builds a sturdy, well-constructed nest of sticks, sited in a substantial tree. Curiously, nests occasionally include, or are decorated with, nests of tent caterpillars, and may have down from the adults around the rim. Sometimes, small passerines such as Baltimore Orioles and Red-eyed Vireos choose to build their nests within the structure.

Food: The bird has a wide variety of prey, which includes snakes, lizards, baby turtles, frogs and toads, fledgling and small birds, small mammals, and even insects.

Range: The Red-shouldered Hawk occurs from southern Canada, down through the eastern United States, and into Central Mexico. There is also an isolated western population, found along the river valleys of California and southern Oregon.

Movements: The most northerly populations migrate south to New Jersey and beyond, with some birds reaching as far south as Central Mexico.

Broad-winged Hawk
Buteo platypterus

Length: 14 - 19in

Wing: 9.5 - 11.5in

Weight: 14 - 16oz

Eggs: 2 - 3 (4); whitish, with bold brownish markings

Incubation: 21 - 25 days

Fledging: 35 - 40 days

Identification: The upperside is dark grayish brown, with the blackish tail showing narrow basal and broader central bands and a dusky tip. The white throat has dark central and lateral streaks, while the rest of the off-white underparts are heavily mottled and barred with rufous brown. The eye is reddish, and the legs and feet are yellow. There is also a rare dark phase.

Habitat: The species is an inhabitant of extensive mixed and broad-leaved forests, and is rarely found in smaller tracts of woodland.

Nest: A variety of trees, both deciduous and coniferous, are chosen for the rather small, poorly-built nest of sticks. It may be lined with bark, and some green sprigs, and is sited anywhere between 3 and 90 feet above the ground.

Food: Snakes, frogs, toads, small mammals, and insects, including large caterpillars, form the main prey of the Broad-winged Hawk; it rarely takes birds, although some individuals seem to specialize in preying on nestlings. The species is also recorded as taking arthropods, crustaceans, and earthworms.

Range: The species ranges across northern North America, from central Alberta and Nova Scotia, down through the eastern United States as far as Texas and Florida.

Movements: Broad-winged Hawks migrate south for the winter, ranging from the Florida Keys, through Mexico, and as far south as Peru and Brazil. In fall, this species arrives simultaneously with Swainson's Hawk over Central America, the vast numbers of both species forming one of the most spectacular sights of the ornithological world.

Short-tailed Hawk

Buteo brachyurus

Length:	17in	**Eggs:**	? ; dull white, usually brown-blotched
Wing:	11 - 13in	**Incubation:**	not recorded
Weight:	12.5+oz	**Fledging:**	not recorded

Identification: The upperparts are dark brownish black, with some white around the base of the bill; the tail is more gray, with a narrow off-white tip and several blackish bands. In contrast, the underparts are white throughout. There is also a sooty-black phase which, however, retains the brown eye, black bill, and yellow legs of the normal form.

Habitat: Most commonly the bird is found in mangroves and cypress swamps, although it sometimes occurs among conifers, and even in open country. In Mexico, it is known from wooded ridges up to about 6,500 feet.

Nest: The nest is rather small for the size of the bird, and is made of sticks, with a lining of twigs and greenery. All nests recorded to date have been in Florida, ranging from 8 to 90 feet above the ground, most often sited in cypresses.

Food: Birds, small rodents, and occasionally insects, seem to be the favored food of the Short-tailed Hawk. In addition, two birds from Panama were discovered to have eaten large lizards.

Range: The bird is found, though not very commonly, in southern Florida and central and southern Mexico.

Movements: More northerly Florida birds move south in the fall, the population becoming concentrated toward the southern tip of the state; the Mexican population, however, appears to be nonmigratory.

Swainson's Hawk
Buteo swainsoni

Length:	19 - 22in	**Eggs:**	2 (3 - 4); white, often weakly
Wing:	14.5 - 17in		marked with brown
Weight:	1lb 15oz -	**Incubation:**	28 days
	2lb 4oz	**Fledging:**	30 days

Identification: This rather variable species is usually dark blackish brown above, and dirty-white below, with the breast brownish, and dark barring and mottling on the remainder of

the underparts. The tail is usually gray, narrowly banded with white at the tip, and with several indistinct dark bands. Both dark and rufous phases occur, and there are numerous intermediary variations between the principal color forms.
Habitat: Open plains and prairies, at low to moderate elevations, are the normal habitat of this species.
Nest: As there are relatively few trees in the bird's habitat, the rather large nest is always conspicuous. It may be as much as four feet across, and is built of twigs, grasses, and other herbage, with a lining of bark, greenery, and sometimes flowers, combined with the bird's own down and feathers. It is sited as high as possible, and some nests have been recorded at heights approaching 100 feet.
Food: The species prefers to feed on large insects, such as orthopterans (crickets and grasshoppers), but small rodents, reptiles, and amphibians, as well as bats and even young or injured birds, also form part of its diet.
Range: The species is found throughout the Great Plains and drier areas of western North America, as far north as Alaska.
Movements: Swainson's Hawk makes the longest and probably the most spectacular fall migration flight of any North American bird species. It moves south in huge numbers to the pampas of Argentina, and where its passage is channelled through Central America, flocks - often in company with large numbers of Broadwings - often take well over an hour to pass. Recently, considerable numbers of mostly immature birds have been overwintering in southern Florida.

White-tailed Hawk
Buteo albicaudatus

Length:	23 - 24in	**Eggs:**	2 (1 - 3); white, sparsely brown-spotted
Wing:	15 - 18in	**Incubation:**	not recorded
Weight:	not recorded	**Fledging:**	not recorded

Identification: The gray upperside, with its contrasting rusty shoulder-patch, and the whitish tail with a single black subterminal band and several thin, wavy brown bars, easily identify this species. The underside is white, with some inconspicuous brown barring. The eye is hazel, and the legs and feet yellow.

Habitat: This tropical and subtropical species is a bird of open and semi-open grasslands, and thinly-wooded areas.

Nest: The species builds a large nest of freshly-broken, often thorny, twigs, mixed with dry grass, and lined with finer, often green, material. It is sited in a sizable bush or small tree, these usually being the only sites available, and therefore is normally no more than 5 to 15 feet above the ground.

Food: Rabbits seem to form the major part of the species' diet, although Cotton Rats, snakes, lizards, frogs and insects, and the occasional bird, are also taken. It has also been recorded as preying on domestic fowl, and even occasionally resorting to carrion.

Range: The species is found in southern Texas, and locally in Mexico.

Movements: The White-tailed Hawk may be a partial migrant southward from Texas into Mexico and South America, but this has yet to be proved.

Zone-tailed Hawk

Buteo albonotatus

Length:	18 - 22in	**Eggs:**	2 (1 - 3); white or bluish-white, unmarked
Wing:	15 - 17in	**Incubation:**	not recorded
Weight:	not recorded	**Fledging:**	not recorded

Identification: This species is deep slaty black all over, with the tail showing a gray tip and two narrow gray bands; a similar basal band is not usually visible. The eye is deep red-brown, and the legs and feet are yellow.

Habitat: This is a bird of mid-altitude mountain slopes (in the southwestern United States) and pine-oak woodlands (in Mexico).

Nest: The birds build a rather bulky and untidy nest of sticks, decorated with greenery. It is placed in any suitable tree, between 25 and 100 feet from the ground, and may be well concealed among the foliage.

Food: The claim that Zone-tailed Hawks feed on frogs and small fishes has yet to be proved. One bird is known to have eaten a chipmunk, while another had taken a small bird and a lizard, and the species is known to snatch nestlings, while in flight.

Range: The species is distributed from western Texas, through New Mexico into central and southern Arizona, down into the mountainous parts of northern Mexico, and then locally southwards into South America.

Movements: In fall, the U.S. populations are partially migratory, moving southwards into Mexico where they join local resident birds which have moved down into the lowlands.

Red-tailed Hawk

Buteo jamaicensis

Length:	19 - 25in	**Eggs:**	1 - 3 (4); whitish, with some dark marbling
Wing:	13 - 17in		
Weight:	2lb 4oz - 2lb 10oz	**Incubation:**	28 - 32 days
		Fledging:	45 days

T. BOYER.

Identification: This highly variable species is usually dark brown above, variegated with rufous and white, and whitish with some dark streaking below. However, the bird's most striking feature, from which it derives its name, is its reddish tail, which has a narrow white tip and a black subterminal band. The eye is brown, and the legs and feet are yellow.

Habitat: The Red-tailed Hawk chooses a wide variety of habitats, from woods and forests interspersed with clear areas, to prairies and drier open areas. It seems to shun extensive timber country.

Nest: The large nest of twigs, with a lining of finer material, is most often built in a tall tree, but where circumstances dictate, the birds choose a rock ledge or a large cactus.

Food: The Red-tailed Hawk takes a wide variety of prey, including mammals up to the size of rabbits and chipmunks, snakes, lizards, and ground-living birds, as well as insects. Occasionally it will prey on creatures too heavy for it to carry away.

Range: The commonest of all North American hawks, the Red-tail is distributed from Alaska and Canada right down through the U.S.A. to Mexico, and into western Panama.

Movements: Populations in the most northerly parts of the range are migratory, moving south to the central United States in large numbers in fall, although some birds always remain, even in snow-bound locations.

Rough-legged Hawk
Buteo lagopus

Length:	20 - 24in	**Eggs:**	3 - 4 (6); white, with
Wing:	15.5 - 19in		brown markings
Weight:	1lb 15oz -	**Incubation:**	28 - 31 days
	2lb 6oz	**Fledging:**	41 days

Identification: The head is whitish brown, with the back somewhat darker brown, and the tail is white, with many black bars, the subterminal one being rather broader. Below, it is dusky-white with dark brown mottling, and usually with a dark belly band. There is a strongly marked dark patch on the underside of the wing at the carpal joint. The feathered tarsi, from which the species derives its name, are barred whitish and brown. There is also a rather uncommon dark phase.

Habitat: The Rough-legged Hawk is a bird of open country and mountainsides, and frequents timber country only if it contains many open areas.

Nest: Normally sited on a rock ledge under an overhang, but occasionally in a tree, the nest is a small structure of twigs of dwarf willow and other arctic plants, with a deep greenery-lined cup. The pair has several alternative nests which are used in annual rotation. The location of a nest is often betrayed by a patch of extra bright green vegetation below, due to the fertilizing effect of food waste and droppings from above.

Food: Small mammals up to the size of rabbits form the bulk of the species' diet, with lemmings being particularly favored in the Arctic. When mammals are in short supply, it preys more on birds. Most food is taken from the ground, and may be located variously by watching from a perch, quartering the ground, or quite often by hovering. Prey is sometimes seized from the surface of water or very wet marshy ground.

Range: The species breeds across Alaska and Canada between latitudes 76° N and 61° N, and is also found right across Eurasia within roughly the same limits.

Movements: In fall the birds migrate south, and during winter may be found over much of the U.S., and occasionally the extreme northern parts of Mexico. The extent of its winter movements is strongly affected by fluctuations in food supply. Years of lemming abundance cause it to stay longer in the breeding areas, and travel less far from them. Rough-legged Hawks sometimes gather before migration, and spend some time soaring about together before leaving in a large group. Migrating birds avoid crossing large sheets of open water, and up to 1,000 a day have been seen passing along the shore of Lake Superior.

Ferruginous Hawk
Buteo regalis

Length: 23 - 24in   **Eggs:**   3 - 4 (5); bluish-white, blotched with brown

Wing: 17in   **Incubation:** 28 days

Weight: not recorded   **Fledging:** 55 - 60 days

Identification: The head and nape are white, with bold blackish-brown streaks; the rest of the upperparts are rufous with blackish brown streaking, and the tail is dusky silver-white, tinged rufous towards the tip. The underparts are white with rusty markings on the belly, and the thighs are barred rufous and black. The eye is pale yellow, and the legs and feet are bright yellow. Rare black and rufous phases have been recorded.

Habitat: This is a species of dry open country, where it is becoming scarce.

Nest: The highest available site in a tree or bush, or among hillside boulders, is selected for the large nest of sticks, lined with cow or horse dung, together with roots and even bleached buffalo bones. The nest is used, and added to, for many years, and can become as much as 12 or 15 feet high.

Food: Small to medium-sized mammals form the bulk of the species' diet, together with some birds, and the occasional snake. When numerous, swarming insects such as crickets and locusts are taken in large numbers.

Range: The Ferruginous Hawk is distributed throughout western North America, from eastern Washington, southern Alberta, southern Saskatchewan, and southwestern Manitoba, down to western Oklahoma, northwestern Texas, and northern Mexico.

Movements: In most, but not all, years, birds from the north of the range migrate south, to winter in northern Mexico and the southwestern United States, south of a line from Manitoba across Montana to South Dakota.

Harpy Eagle
Harpia harpyja

Length:	34 - 37in	**Eggs:**	2; white, soon becoming heavily yellow-stained
Wing:	21.5 - 24in	**Incubation:**	not recorded
Weight ♂:	8 - 10lbs	**Fledging:**	not recorded

Identification: The Harpy Eagle is unmistakable, not only on account of its size, but also on account of its divided crest of blackish erectile crown feathers. The head is ash-gray, while the back is blackish-gray with paler marbling. The tail is black, with three broad, gray bars and a narrow tip of the same color. Below, the bird is white with a black collar, and dark barring on the thighs. The massive legs and feet are yellow, and the eye is pale brown.

Habitat: This is a bird of low- and mid-altitude virgin tropical forest, where, despite its size, it is surprisingly inconspicuous.

Nest: Our limited knowledge of the Harpy Eagle's nest is based on just two study sites in southern Guyana. The nest is a large structure, up to four feet thick by five feet across, built with sticks up to 1.5 inches in diameter, and with a deep cup lined with green leaves and animal hair. It is placed in a massive tree, at heights in excess of 150 feet, and is apparently used for many years; in fact, it seems probable that the young are dependent on the parents for such a long time that most nests are used only every other year.

Food: It seems that the bird's main prey are tree-living mammals such as sloths and monkeys. It is thought that large birds, as well as snakes, and terrestrial mammals such as agoutis, are also taken at times.

Range: Although primarily a species of northern South America, Harpies are sometimes reported from Veracruz, Chiapas, and Campeche in southern Mexico.

Movements: Harpy Eagles are strictly nonmigratory.

Golden Eagle

Aquila chrysaetos

Length:	30 - 35in	**Eggs:**	2; dull white, blotched red-brown and gray
Wing:	22.5 - 28in		
Weight ♂:	7 - 9lbs	**Incubation:**	45 days
Weight ♀:	8 - 12lbs	**Fledging:**	80 days

Identification: The entire upperside is dark brown (paler in some individuals), with the lanceolate crown and nape feathers edged with gold. The tail has a number of irregular dark gray bands. Below, the bird is somewhat paler brown than above, with the thigh feathering some shade of buff, and the legs and feet yellow.

Habitat: This is a bird of the most inhospitable and extensive open mountainous areas of the Northern Hemisphere, and this is especially true in the United States.

Nest: The untidy nest of sticks and branches is most often sited on a rocky crag (although occasionally in a tree), and over the course of many seasons it can become enormous. Most pairs have a number of alternative sites, which are used in rotation.

Food: The Golden Eagle preys on a wide variety of mammals up to the size of a small deer fawn, and some gamebirds, all invariably taken on the ground. It undoubtedly does eat domestic lambs, and even sheep, on occasion, but in such cases the prey is probably already dead, or at least extremely sick.

Range: The species ranges over almost all of North America, from Alaska and southern Canada down to Central Mexico.

Movements: The Golden Eagle is a partial migrant, with individuals from the coldest northerly part of the range moving south for the winter.

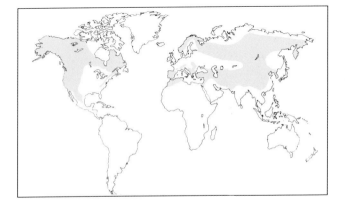

Black and White Hawk-eagle
Spizastur melanoleucus

Length: 22 - 24in **Eggs:** ? 2; white or cream, usually brown-spotted

Wing: 13.5 - 16.5in **Incubation:** not recorded

Weight: 27oz **Fledging:** not recorded

Identification: In this striking species the entire underside is white, as is the head, with the exception of black feathering around the eye, and a short black crest. The upperside is black, becoming browner on the wings, and the tail has three gray bands and a gray tip. The eye and legs are pale yellow.

Habitat: This is a bird of humid tropical forests, with a preference for tree-bordered rivers, as well as clearings and forest edges.

Nest: A nest recently observed in Panama was a large stick structure high in a forest tree; otherwise, nothing at all has been recorded of this bird's breeding habits.

Food: There appear to be no authenticated records of the bird's feeding preferences, but it is generally thought to prey on duck-sized birds, and mammals of similar bulk. In northern Argentina it appears to be confined to the vicinity of rivers, where cormorants and Brazilian Mergansers are reported as prey. However, it is by no means limited to rivers elsewhere, presumably because other prey are available to it.

Range: The species is extremely thinly distributed in southern and southeastern Mexico, and appears to be a casual visitor to Yucatan.

Movements: Our present knowledge suggests that the Black and White Hawk-eagle is nonmigratory.

Black Hawk-eagle

Spizaetus tyrannus

Length: 25 - 28in
Wing: 14 - 17.5in
Weight: 1lb 15oz - 2lb 8oz

Eggs: not recorded

Incubation: not recorded
Fledging: not recorded

Identification: Apart from the black-tipped white crest, the overall plumage is black, with scattered white mottling which forms distinct barring on the thighs and the upper- and under-tail coverts. The tail has three broad gray bars and a gray tip, while the eyes and feet are orange-yellow.

Habitat: The Black Hawk-eagle is a bird of semi-open country, from sea level up to about 6,000 feet.

Nest: So far, the only known nest of this species was some 45 feet up in a palm. It was built of sticks, and judged to be about 4.5 feet across. The adults defended the nest vigorously, screaming and diving at the observer.

Food: Virtually nothing is known of the feeding habits of this species, but it is generally thought to prey on birds, bats, and small arboreal mammals. One record is of a bird seen with two feathered nestlings of a flycatcher clutched in its talons, together with part of their nest. As this is one of the less robustly built hawk-eagles, it probably takes, on average, rather smaller prey than most.

Range: This basically South American species is a rare resident in Mexico, from southern Tamaulipas along the coastal slope to Campeche, and is an occasional visitor to Yucatan.

Movements: There is no evidence to suggest that this species makes any migratory journeys.

Ornate Hawk-eagle

Spizaetus ornatus

Length:	23 - 25in	**Eggs:**	not recorded
Wing:	13.5 - 15.5in		
Weight:	2lb 2oz -	**Incubation:**	not recorded
	3lb 8oz	**Fledging:**	not recorded

Identification: This aptly-named and handsome species has the crown and long erectile crest black, the sides of the head and an incomplete breast band chestnut, and the rest of the upperparts black, with the tail showing three broad gray-marbled bands and a narrow tip of the same coloration. Below, the bird is white, with heavy black barring. The eye is bright orange, and the feet yellow.

Habitat: The species seems to prefer humid tropical forest, interspersed with some open areas, at altitudes up to 8,000 or 9,000 feet.

Nest: The few nests so far discovered have been at least 90 feet up in a tree, and built of sticks up to as much as 4 inches in diameter. The bulk of one nest was estimated at 53 cubic feet. Activity at the nest tends to be accompanied by much loud calling, especially when there are large young in the nest.

Food: The bird's main diet seems to consist of birds ranging in size from quail to small herons; however, it is apparently not averse to taking small mammals. An interesting record was of an Ornate Hawk-eagle seen consuming a Black Vulture near the carcass that had attracted it. Possibly the carcass, a monkey, was a previous victim of the eagle, to which the latter had returned after an interval.

Range: The species is found along the coastal slope of Mexico, from Tamaulipas to Campeche, and occasionally in Yucatan.

Movements: It is doubtful if the Ornate Hawk-eagle makes any migratory flights.

CARACARAS
AND FALCONS

Family FALCONIDAE

Red-throated Caracara

Daptrius americanus

Length:	19 - 22in	**Eggs:**	? 2 - 3; white or buff,
Wing:	14in		spotted with brown
Weight:	1lb 4oz -	**Incubation:**	not recorded
	1lb 11oz	**Fledging:**	not recorded

Identification: The overall plumage is black, glossed with blue and green, but with the thighs, abdomen, and streaks on the sides of the head white. The unfeathered cheeks, throat, and legs are orange-red, and the eye is red-brown.

Habitat: The species inhabits humid tropical and subtropical rainforest, where it is most frequently found in small groups along forest edges and in semi-cleared areas.

Nest: Little seems to have been recorded about the species' breeding habits, but it is thought to build a nest of twigs, sited in a tree.

Food: The Red-throated Caracara feeds almost exclusively on wasp larvae, which it obtains by tearing open the nests of even the most fearsome stinging species. Other recorded food items are caterpillars, fruit, and soft seeds. Great agility is shown when feeding, especially when working on a wasp's nest to create an opening big enough to extract insects: at such times it regularly hangs completely upside-down from the torn edge of the nest. The presence of a foraging party of these caracaras is betrayed by their continual raucous cries. Outside the edge of continuous forest they stay largely in the treetops, and might then go unnoticed but for the amount of noise they make.

Range: The species is locally distributed in southern Mexico, from southern Veracruz to northern Chiapas.

Movements: The Red-throated Caracara is not known to migrate.

Crested Caracara

Polyborus plancus

Length:	20 - 24in	**Eggs:**	2 - 3 (4); white to vinaceous, usually marked reddish-brown
Wing:	14 - 16in		
Weight:	2lb 3oz - 3lb 4oz	**Incubation:**	28 days
		Fledging:	56 - 85 days

Identification: The general plumage is blackish-brown, with a slight crest; the sides of the head, the neck, and the breast are white, with many of the breast and neck feathers tipped brown-black. The belly and tail are off-white, the tail showing several narrow dark bars, and a broad black tip. The bill is whitish, the eye brown, the bare facial skin red, and the long legs yellow.

Habitat: This is a species of both arid and well-watered open or semi-open tropical and subtropical country; indeed, any fairly open habitat in which it can easily find food.

Nest: The nest is a large untidy structure of sticks, which may or may not have a lining of any available soft debris. It is usually sited up to 80 feet high in a dense tree or palm, but sometimes a cactus is chosen. When no other suitable site is available, the nest is sited on the ground.

Food: The species is both predator and scavenger, taking all types of vertebrate and invertebrate food, and possibly some vegetable material.

Range: The Crested Caracara is found in central and southern Florida, and from southern Arizona and Texas southward into most parts of Mexico.

Movements: The species is not known to migrate.

Laughing Falcon
Herpetotheres cachinnans

Length:	18 - 22in	**Eggs:**	1; whitish, with heavy brown markings
Wing:	10 - 12in	**Incubation:**	not recorded
Weight:	14 - 23oz	**Fledging:**	not recorded

Identification: The entire underside and head are buff, the head having black streaking on the crown and a broad black mask extending backward from around the eyes to form a narrow collar on the hind-neck. The rest of the upperside is dark brown, with the tail barred alternately black and white, and with a white tip. The eye is brown, and the legs and feet are pale yellow.

Habitat: The species is most common in semi-open tropical lowlands, although it is also found in dry forested regions, provided there are some clearings.

Nest: No nest is built, the birds selecting either the disused nest of some other species or, more frequently, a cavity or shallow hollow in a tree, at heights varying from 35 to 100 feet.

Food: The species specializes in capturing reptiles, especially snakes, both venomous and nonvenomous, and often surprisingly large. It also takes some invertebrates and small rodents.

Range: The Laughing Falcon is found southward from Central Mexico, along both ocean-facing slopes, but is very scarce in the interior.

Movements: The Laughing Falcon is nonmigratory.

Barred Forest Falcon
Micrastur ruficollis

Length:	13 - 15in	**Eggs:**	not recorded
Wing:	6.5 - 8in	**Incubation:**	not recorded
Weight:	6 - 7oz	**Fledging:**	not recorded

Identification: This rather short-winged and long-tailed falcon is dark slaty-gray above, with the tail showing three very narrow white bars and an equally narrow white tip. Below, the throat is pale gray, and the remainder of the underparts are white, with fine black barring. The eye is orange-brown, and the legs and feet are orange-yellow. The female tends to be browner, with paler eyes and legs.

Habitat: This common but rather unobtrusive small falcon is found in most dense subtropical and tropical forests.

Nest: Surprisingly, although it is a fairly common species, details of the Barred Forest Falcon's breeding habits seem not to have been recorded.

Food: Forest Falcons have short, rounded wings, ideal for weaving their way at high speed through trees and lianas, and they thus resemble hawks of the genus *Accipiter* in their general habits, though not quite so bold and dashing. A common tactic of the present species is to dash at a party of birds from cover and attempt to seize one. When seeking prey, it typically perches low in the forest, concealed by vegetation. It specializes particularly in attacking birds that have gathered to feed on columns of army ants. Lizards and mice are also included in its diet. It is regularly active well into twilight.

Range: In Mexico, the species is distributed south and east from Puebla through to the southern part of the Yucatan Peninsula.

Movements: There is no evidence to suggest that the species makes any migratory movements.

Collared Forest Falcon
Micrastur semitorquatus

Length:	18 - 24in	**Eggs:**	not recorded
Wing:	10 - 11in	**Incubation:**	not recorded
Weight:	18 - 26.5oz	**Fledging:**	not recorded

Identification: The upperside is deep black, with a white collar; the black of the crown extends down the sides of the head, and the rear edge of the face is marked by a black crescentic mark. The rest of the face, and the entire underside, are unmarked white, while the tail has at least three narrow white bars, and a white tip. The eye is dark brown, and the legs and feet are pale yellow. Tawny and dark phases are also known. The bird's prominent eyes, large ear-openings, and facial ruff appear to be adaptations to its crepuscular way of life.

Habitat: This striking species is an inhabitant of dense tropical forest, up to levels of about 7,000 feet, where it seems to prefer dense, almost impenetrable, vegetation, including mangroves. It is extraordinarily adept at moving through such dense cover with agility and at high speed, both on the wing and on foot.

Nest: The species' nest appears never to have been found, and we know nothing of its breeding cycle.

Food: The speed and agility of this bold and aggressive hunter allow it to take a variety of birds (including the occasional domestic fowl), small mammals, lizards, snakes, and large insects.

Range: The species' Mexican distribution extends south down both coastal slopes, from Sinaloa in the west, and from southern Tamaulipas to the Yucatan Peninsula in the east.

Movements: The species appears to be nonmigratory.

American Kestrel
Falco sparverius

Length:	10.5in	**Eggs:**	4 (3 - 7); white to pale pink, heavily brown-marked
Wing:	6.5 - 8in	**Incubation:**	29 - 30 days
Weight:	3.8 - 4.2oz	**Fledging:**	30 days

Identification: The slate-gray crown is partly bordered with black, and often has a central rufous patch. The rufous back is flecked with black, while the plain rufous tail has a black terminal band and a narrow white tip. The wings are blue-gray with scattered black markings, and the primaries are black. The

cheeks, bordered by two vertical black bars, and the throat, are white; the rest of the underparts are varying shades of rufous, becoming paler toward the tail, and with black spotting in the lower regions. The eye is brown, and the legs and feet are orange-yellow. The female is less colorful, with rufous replacing much of the gray, and more extensive black spotting on the back and tail, where the terminal band is much narrower.

Habitat: The only indigenous American kestrel, this attractive little falcon is found in all types of open country, preferably where there are some trees, as well as in suburbs, and even city centers.

Nest: The species builds no nest, choosing instead to lay its eggs in any suitable cavity in a tree, rock-face or even a building. Occasionally, the birds will use the disused nest of some other species.

Food: The American Kestrel's main diet consists of large insects, particularly grasshoppers, but when these are not available it preys on mice and small birds, and occasionally on lizards, scorpions, and amphibians. The bird has also been known to prey on swarms of small bats.

Range: The species ranges from the tree-line of Alaska and Canada, south through the entire United States into northern and western Mexico, and down to the extreme south of South America.

Movements: Birds breeding north of about 40°N migrate south in fall, along with some more southerly-breeding birds, to winter in southern Florida and many parts of Mexico.

Eurasian Kestrel
Falco tinnunculus

Length:	13 - 14in	**Eggs:**	4 (2 - 6); white to yellowish,
Wing:	8.5 - 11in		heavily marked red-brown
Weight ♂: 4 - 8oz		**Incubation:**	28 days
Weight ♀: 6 - 9.5oz		**Fledging:**	28 - 30 days

Identification: The crown and nape are gray, with black shaft-streaks, while the rest of the upperparts are chestnut, marked with black pear-shaped spots of varying sizes. The primaries are deep black-brown. The face has a dark moustachial stripe, and

the underparts are buff, spotted with black-brown. The blue-gray tail has a broad black subterminal band and a narrow white tip, and the legs are yellow. The female lacks the gray on the head and tail, is more heavily spotted, and has many narrow black bars across the tail.

Habitat: This is a bird of open tree-scattered country from sea level up to at least 15,000 feet, but it is absent from densely-forested areas, higher mountain regions, and harsh deserts.

Nest: No nest is built. A cavity or hollow in a tree is a common breeding site, but similar situations among rocks, and in or on man-made structures such as buildings, bridges, pylons, and even bale-ricks are equally acceptable, as are disused nests of other species such as crows (Corvidae). Due to this variety of sites, the nest may be at any level, from a few feet above ground to over 100.

Food: The species' main prey consists of small mammals, but it will also take small to medium-sized birds, lizards, small snakes, frogs, and a variety of insects.

Range: A species found over much of Europe, Asia, and Africa, the Eurasian Kestrel occurs as a casual or accidental winter visitor to the western Aleutians and the east coast of the United States. Birds seen elsewhere on the American continent are most likely to be escaped falconers' birds.

Movements: Birds breeding in Eastern Europe and Central Asia are highly migratory, moving south to warmer parts for the winter; however, sometimes individuals from apparently non-migratory populations also travel considerable distances in fall.

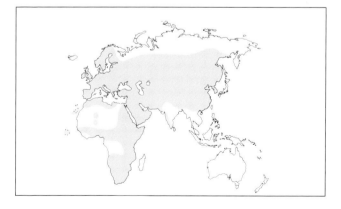

Merlin
Falco columbarius

Length:	10.5 - 13in	**Eggs:**	6 (2 - 7); pale buff, heavily
Wing:	7.5 - 9in		marked red-brown
Weight ♂:	5 - 7.5oz	**Incubation:**	28 - 32 days
Weight ♀:	6.5 - 9oz	**Fledging:**	25 - 30 days

Identification: The upperparts are slate-blue, darker on the crown, with fine black streaking throughout; there is also an indistinct dark moustachial stripe, and a broad rufous collar. The tail has a dark subterminal band, and a pale gray tip. Below, the plumage is pale rufous, marked with black-brown

streaks and spots, and the legs are yellow. The female is browner, lacking much of the gray tone of the male, but has more tail bands.

Habitat: The tiny, fast-flying Merlin is a bird of thinly-wooded or open country, including the sea-shore, marshlands, grasslands, and deserts. It frequents forested regions only if they also provide open hunting areas.

Nest: Most often, the nest is a ground-scrape, usually in dense low vegetation, but sometimes a bulky nest of grasses and other stems is formed, probably by the incubating bird plucking material from the immediate surroundings. In woodland, the birds usually take over the disused nests of species such as crows (Corvidae), and may be anywhere between 5 and 60 feet above the ground.

Food: The Merlin is a bold hunter of birds, occasionally rather bigger than itself, but it also takes some small mammals, lizards, snakes, and insects, especially dragonflies.

Range: The bird's breeding range extends north from northern California across to Newfoundland, as far as the tree limit in Canada and Alaska. In winter, it is found throughout most of central and southern U.S.A., and Mexico.

Movements: In fall the species migrates south to winter in the southern United States, along the sea coasts of Mexico, and even as far south as the West Indies, Venezuela, and Ecuador.

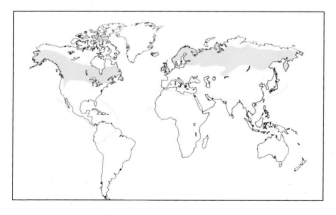

Bat Falcon
Falco rufigularis

Length: 9 - 12in
Wing: 7 - 9in
Weight ♂: 3.8 - 5oz
Weight ♀: 6 - 8.5oz

Eggs: 3 (2 - 4); rich brown, with dense darker speckling
Incubation: not recorded
Fledging: 35 - 40 days

Identification: The crown, the sides of the head, and the entire back, including the tail, are sooty black, with the tail showing several narrow grayish bars and narrow white tip. The throat, sides of the neck, and upper breast are white, often washed with tawny. Much of the rest of the underparts are black, narrowly marked with white, while the lower belly and thighs are chestnut. The legs and feet are bright yellow.

Habitat: The Bat Falcon is found in humid tropical woodland areas, up to about 5,000 feet, where it is frequently seen perched along woodland edges, in clearings, or alongside roads.

Nest: The nest is most often a suitable tree cavity or open hollow, perhaps as high as 100 feet, the eggs being laid directly on the floor among any already-accumulated debris. Sometimes the birds will use a ledge on a cliff-face, or even a man-made structure.

Food: As its name implies, the Bat Falcon specializes in preying on bats, though it also takes small birds, such as swallows, swifts, and humming birds, as well as flying insects, all captured on the wing.

Range: In Mexico, the species is rather rare along the Pacific slope, from southeast Sonora to Chiapas, but it is more common along the Gulf slope, from southern Tamaulipas to the Yucatan Peninsula.

Movements: Bat Falcons are strictly nonmigratory.

Aplomado Falcon
Falco femoralis

Length:	15 - 18in	**Eggs:**	2 - 3 (4); white or pinkish-white, with brown spots and blotches
Wing:	10 - 12in	**Incubation:**	not recorded
Weight:	8oz	**Fledging:**	not recorded

Identification: The upperparts are bluish-gray, interrupted by a buff-white stripe running round the back of the head from behind the eyes. The throat and cheeks are buff-white, with a dark moustachial stripe. The buff breast is separated from the tawny belly and thighs by a more or less complete band of white-tipped black feathers, and the white-tipped, almost black tail is crossed by several narrow white bars. The eye color varies from yellowish to dark brown, and the legs are deep yellow.

Habitat: This is a bird of open country with scattered trees and cacti, and of woodland and light forest.

Nest: The species always lays its eggs in disused stick nests of other species.

Food: Flying birds and insects are main prey of the Aplomado Falcon, but it is also known to take small terrestrial mammals and lizards.

Range: Although the species formerly had a much greater North American range, it is now rare, and restricted to the southwestern United States, parts of northern and northwestern Mexico, and eastern Mexico from Tamaulipas to the Yucatan Peninsula.

Movements: In fall, birds breeding in the United States and northern Mexico migrate to southern Mexico, and possibly further south, to join the much larger South American population.

Prairie Falcon
Falco mexicanus

Length: 15.5 - 19.5in **Eggs:** 4 - 5 (3 - 6); white to pinkish-white, heavily spotted and blotched with brown or purple

Wing: 11.5 - 14in **Incubation:** 29 - 31 days
Weight: 28oz **Fledging:** 40 days

Identification: The crown, the sides of the head, the back, and the white-tipped tail, are all brown, with many of the back feathers light-edged, and the outer tail feathers buff-barred. A weak line over the brown eye, a faint collar, and the cheeks, are all whitish, and there is an ill-defined brown moustachial stripe. The white throat merges into the creamy-white underparts, which are boldly marked with elongated brown spots. The legs are yellow.

Habitat: The species is found in inland arid steppes and plains up to about 1,200 feet, provided there are cliffs of rocky outcrops suitable for nesting.

Nest: The birds always nest on cliffs, usually selecting a ledge with an overhang, a pothole, or a cave, and making a slight scrape for the eggs. Alternatively, the old nest of some other species is used. Sites average about 35 feet above the cliff base.

Food: The species preys on small to medium-sized birds and mammals, supplemented with lizards and large insects. Almost all prey is captured on the ground.

Range: The Prairie Falcon occurs throughout the western half of North America, from central British Columbia to Saskatchewan in Canada, and western North Dakota south to Arizona, New Mexico and Texas, and down into Mexico.

Movements: The species is a partial migrant, with some birds wintering as far south as Mexico, while others, even in Canada, remain on their breeding grounds throughout the year.

Gyrfalcon
Falco rusticolus

Length: 20 - 24in
Wing: 13.5 - 16.5in
Weight ♂: 2lb 1oz - 2lb 14oz
Weight ♀: 3lb 1oz - 4lb 6oz

Eggs: 4 (2 - 7); white to buff, usually spotted red
Incubation: 28 - 29 days
Fledging: 46 - 49 days

Identification: The Gyrfalcon is extremely variable, with no two individuals exactly alike, and females usually darker than males. Generally, the upperparts are gray-brown to gray, lighter on the head, and much checkered with whitish on the back, while the white-tipped tail is usually alternately barred light and dark. The underparts are white, with dark brown spots, increasing in size and number toward the tail. The eye is dark brown, and the powerful legs and feet are yellow. Plumage variants range from almost unmarked white, to an all-over deep charcoal brown, but the bird's size and powerful build should confirm its identity.

Habitat: The wild, remote Arctic mountains and wastelands are the usual habitat of this species, although it may occasionally occur in lightly wooded areas along the northern limit of the tree line.

Nest: Gyrfalcons build no nest: the eggs are usually laid on an overhung cliff-ledge, but the birds will also use old nests of species such as Rough-legged Buzzards and Ravens, even when these are in trees.

Food: This powerful predator feeds mainly on birds, ranging in size from small songbirds to geese. Ptarmigan form the greater part of its diet, although in some areas seabirds are taken in large numbers, while small mammals become more important in its winter quarters.

Range: The Gyrfalcon is mainly distributed across arctic Alaska and Canada, north of the tree line, but may be seen, chiefly in winter, as far south as the extreme north of the United States.

Movements: Although some birds remain on their breeding grounds throughout the year, many (mostly immatures) move south as far as latitude 45°N for the winter.

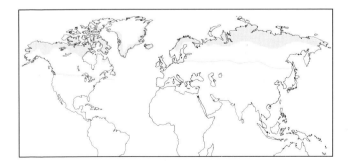

Orange-breasted Falcon
Falco deiroleucus

Length: 13 - 15in   **Eggs:** 2 - 3; buff, heavily speckled red-brown
Wing: 10 - 11.5in
Weight ♂: 12oz   **Incubation:** not recorded
Weight ♀: 19 - 23oz   **Fledging:** not recorded

Identification: The entire upperparts, including the face, are black, with many of the feathers edged slaty-gray. The white of the throat extends to form an incomplete collar, merging with the orange-brown underparts, which are interupted by a more or less complete broad band of black, mixed with orange-buff and dirty white. The tail is crossed by four very narrow white bars, and the legs and feet are bright yellow.

Habitat: This rather rare species inhabits cool, moist mountain forest up to 7,500 feet.

Nest: The nest of the Orange-breasted Falcon has yet to be positively identified. Some observers maintain that the bird nests in ruins and church towers, while a nest in a stick-filled hollow at the base of a palm frond was also claimed to belong to this species. Generally, it is believed to nest in cavities in large trees, or holes in rocky cliff faces.

Food: The Orange-breasted Falcon probably specializes in hunting birds: the only recorded prey items are doves, caciques, and parrots.

Range: In Mexico, the species has been recorded only from Vera Cruz and Chiapas, although its South American range extends to Peru and northern Argentina.

Movements: Present knowledge of the species indicates no migratory tendencies.

Peregrine Falcon
Falco peregrinus

Length:	14 - 19in	**Eggs:**	2 - 5 (6); creamy,
Wing:	10.5 - 15in		heavily marked red-brown
Weight ♂:	1lb 3oz -	**Incubation:**	28 - 29 days
	1lb 6oz		
Weight ♀:	1lb 10oz -	**Fledging:**	35 - 42 days
	2lb 8oz		

Identification: The upperparts are dark slaty blue, becoming almost black on the head, where the darker color extends down the sides to form a "helmet". The underparts are white on the chin, becoming gradually darker buff toward the tail, and becoming more heavily spotted and barred with black in the same direction. The tail is barred alternately blue-gray and black, with a dirty-white tip. The legs and feet are bright yellow. The female is often darker, with pear-shaped spots on the breast, and heavier barring. There is considerable variation in size and color, the species becoming gradually smaller and darker from north to south of its range.

Habitat: Although the Peregrine Falcon is associated mainly with cliffs and rocky crags, most commonly along coasts, it is also found in both forested and open country, including grasslands and moorland, up to at least 10,000 feet.

Nest: Usually an inaccessible rocky ledge or hole, with a slight scrape for the eggs. Uncommon alternatives are the disused stick nest of some other species, a hollow tree-trunk or limb, or even a ledge on a tall building.

Food: The species preys almost exclusively on birds, ranging in size from small passerines up to wild duck, with pigeons (Columbidae) being specially favored, but a few mammals, amphibians, and even insects are also taken.

Range: Though far less common than in earlier times, the bird is still to be found toward the coasts of northern Canada, the eastern and western United States, and Mexico.

Movements: The most northerly populations migrate in fall to overwinter in the southeast of the United States, and the coastal regions of Mexico.

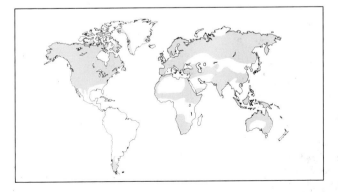

Index